HEALTH HEROES

I'M A NURSE

LAUREN KUKLA

ILLUSTRATED BY **NADIA GUNAWAN**

MAYO CLINIC PRESS KIDS

With gratitude to Josh Vu, RN

MAYO CLINIC PRESS KIDS | An imprint of Mayo Clinic Press
200 First St. SW
Rochester, MN 55905
MCPress.MayoClinic.org

To stay informed about Mayo Clinic Press, please subscribe to our free e-newsletter at MCPress.MayoClinic.org or follow us on social media.

The medical information in this book is true and complete to the best of our knowledge. This book is intended as an informative guide for those wishing to learn more about health issues. It is not intended to replace, countermand or conflict with advice given to you by your own physician. The ultimate decision concerning your care should be made between you and your doctor. Information in this book is offered with no guarantees. The author and publisher disclaim all liability in connection with the use of this book. The views expressed are the author's personal views, and do not necessarily reflect the policy or position of Mayo Clinic.

For bulk sales contact Mayo Clinic at SpecialSalesMayoBooks@mayo.edu.

Proceeds from the sale of every book benefit important medical research and education at Mayo Clinic.

ISBN: 9798887700731 (paperback) | 9798887700724 (library binding) | 9798887701516 (ebook) | 9798887701226 (multiuser PDF) | 9798887700748 (multiuser ePub)

Library of Congress Control Number: 2023024579
Library of Congress Cataloging-in-Publication Data is available upon request.

TABLE OF CONTENTS

CHAPTER 1

HELLO!

Hello! My name is Manny Gutierrez. I'm a pediatric nurse! A pediatric nurse takes care of young people.

My job is special because I get to take care of the bravest kids in the world.

Most pediatric nurses work in hospitals or **clinics**. I work in the general pediatric unit of a hospital. The doctors and nurses in my unit are specially trained to care for kids. Some of our patients are sick or injured. Others stay with us before and after a **surgery**.

HOSPITAL

CHAPTER 2

A NURSE'S TOOL KIT

Being a nurse takes special skills. Nurses need to have respect, empathy, and compassion. We need to be able to think on our feet. But there are also tools that help me do my job.

VITAL SIGNS MONITOR

Displays heart rate, blood pressure, and other important information about patients' health

PULSE OXIMETER

Measures oxygen levels in the blood

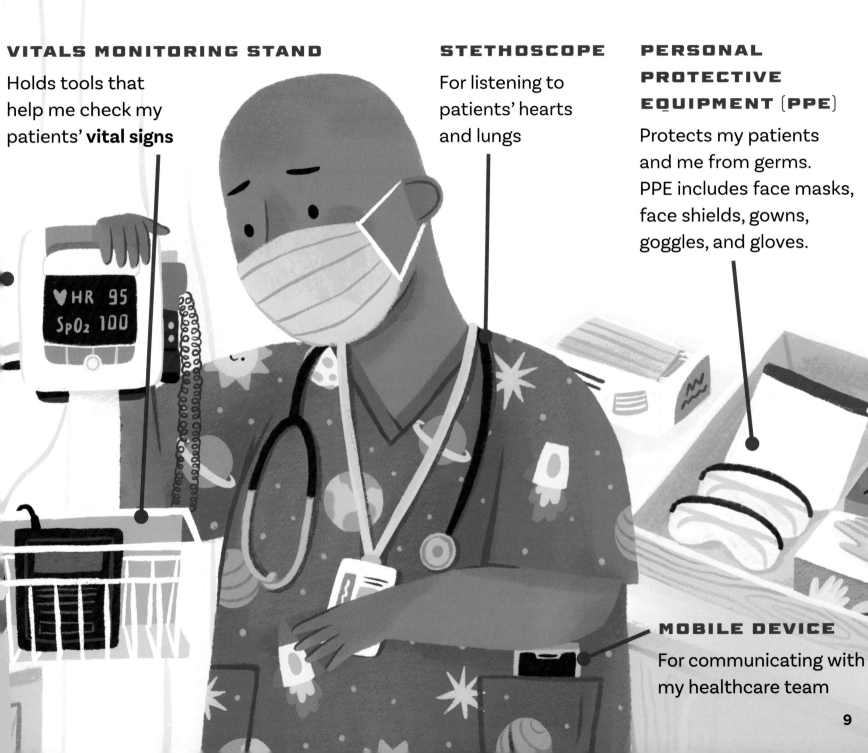

VITALS MONITORING STAND

Holds tools that help me check my patients' **vital signs**

♥ HR 95
SpO₂ 100

STETHOSCOPE

For listening to patients' hearts and lungs

PERSONAL PROTECTIVE EQUIPMENT (PPE)

Protects my patients and me from germs. PPE includes face masks, face shields, gowns, goggles, and gloves.

MOBILE DEVICE

For communicating with my healthcare team

9

I work with different nurses, doctors, and other members of my healthcare team to keep our patients healthy and safe. **Meet some of the people on the team!**

DR. OKOYE
PHYSICIAN
Treats patients

JUSTIN
PHYSICAL THERAPIST
Helps patients with their movement after an injury or surgery

ROSA
INTERPRETER
Translates for patients who speak another language

CHAPTER 3

A DAY AS A NURSE

I usually work a twelve-hour **shift**. Sometimes I work all night! But today, my shift starts in the morning.

6:50 AM

Before I enter the hospital, I put on my ID badge. Inside, I change into scrubs and take the elevator up to the general pediatric floor.

I look over my patient assignments on my computer. I meet with the night shift nurse. Then I make a plan for how to best care for my patients.

7:20 AM

I visit each of my patients' rooms. I say good morning and tell them my name if I haven't met them yet. I let them know I will be taking care of them for the next twelve hours. Today, I meet Josh. He was in a bike accident and broke his leg.

14

9:30 AM

Ava is being treated for cancer. Cancer treatments can be very hard on a person's body. Ava is staying at the hospital to recover from her last treatment. I check Ava's vital signs.

10:00
AM

Isaac is sick with an **infection**. He also has **diabetes**. I give him **insulin** to help manage his diabetes. I give him an **antibiotic** to help his body heal from the infection.

16

11:15
AM

Ariana has **RSV**. I monitor her breathing. I give her oxygen. Then Rosa and I answer some questions Ariana's parents have about RSV. Nurses often help teach patients and their families about their healthcare!

1:30
PM

I bring Josh to the physical therapy gym to see Justin. Justin teaches Josh how to walk on crutches.

2:30 PM

Isaac's mom told me he is a chess whiz. I bring in a chessboard so we can play a few moves each hour when I check on him.

4:00 PM

Dr. Okoye lets me know that Ariana gets to go home! She asks me to bring some **discharge** papers to her family.

5:00 PM

Rosa and I meet with Ariana's family. We make sure they know how to care for her at home. We ask them to follow up with Ariana's primary care doctor in a few days.

6:00 PM

I enter notes about my patients into the computer.

6:50 PM

I meet with the night shift nurse, Jameelah. She will be taking care of my patients on the next shift. I update her on my patients' care.

23

CHAPTER 4

PATIENTS COME FIRST

I wrap up every shift the same way. I visit each of my patients one last time. I thank them for letting me care for them. I introduce them to the nurse who will be taking care of them next.

Being a nurse can be a challenge. My shifts are long. It can be hard to care for kids dealing with serious illnesses and injuries.

Still, I love my job! I have the bravest patients in the world. I feel proud that I get to care for them. At the end of each shift, I know that I've made a difference!

REAL-LIFE HERO!

MEET A REAL-LIFE NURSE!

NAME: Josh Vu

JOB: Pediatric Intensive Care Nurse

PLACE OF WORK: Mayo Clinic

What is your favorite part of being a nurse?

I have the bravest little patients. It is an honor, joy, and privilege to take care of them. Being in a hospital can be a scary time for kids and their families. Helping my patients and their loved ones during this time, and seeing them get better, is extremely rewarding.

What does a nurse do?

I check my patients' vital signs to see how they are doing. This helps me understand how to best care for my patients. I give my patients medicine to help them heal. I play with my patients to ease their fears. I work closely with a team of other healthcare professionals to help my patients. I also look after my patients' family members to make sure they are doing okay.

What is the hardest part about being a nurse?

A pediatric intensive care unit is where some of the hospital's sickest kids are treated. Because of this, I see many difficult circumstances. It is challenging to see children who do not get better. But most of the time, I see great victories for the kids I care for.

What character traits do you think it's important for nurses to have?

Pediatric nurses need to be fun. The hospital can be a scary setting for anyone, but especially for children. A sense of fun helps pediatric nurses create environments where sick children feel safe. We always look for ways to bring smiles to our patients' faces!

SUPERPOWER SPOTLIGHT

Health heroes have special superpowers that help them do their jobs. One of a nurse's most important superpowers is empathy! That means I try to understand how my patients might be feeling. I listen carefully when they are talking to me. I make sure they understand everything that is happening to them. I give them time to ask questions and tell me what they are thinking and feeling. I show all my patients empathy.

HOW DO YOU SHOW EMPATHY?

EMPATHY

GLOSSARY

antibiotic—a medicine that kills bacteria or stops it from growing. Bacteria are tiny living things that are made up of just one cell and can cause disease.

clinic—a healthcare building where patients have scheduled visits with healthcare providers

diabetes—a condition in which the body cannot properly regulate the amount of sugar in the blood

discharge—to release from something, such as a hospital's care

infection—the entry and growth of germs in the human body

insulin—a hormone that lowers the levels of sugar in the blood

RSV—respiratory syncytial virus. RSV is a virus that usually causes mild cold-like symptoms but can sometimes be serious, especially in very young children and older adults.

shift—a scheduled period of time that a person is at work

surgery—a medical procedure where doctors treat or diagnose conditions, usually done after a doctor has given the patient medicine to make them sleep

vital signs—measurements of a patient's basic functions, such as heart rate, blood pressure, and temperature

LEARN MORE

Murray, Julie. *Nurses*. Minneapolis: Abdo Kids, 2021.

Nemours KidsHealth. "Going to the Hospital."
    https://kidshealth.org/en/kids/hospital.html

Slegers, Liesbet. *Nurses and What They Do*. New York: Clavis, 2021.

Waxman, Laura Hamilton. *Nurse Tools*. Minneapolis: Lerner Publications, 2020.

INDEX